BRINGING EFFECTIVE
QUALITY ASSURANCE
INTO A SMALL BUSINESS

BRINGING EFFECTIVE
QUALITY ASSURANCE
INTO A SMALL BUSINESS

A Common Sense Guide to Getting Quality
to Work for the Bottom Line in Your Business

JOHN NOLAND FRYE

ReadersMagnet, LLC

CONTENTS

PREFACE

W HEN I FIRST WROTE THIS BOOK SOME
14 years ago, the ISO standard was 9001-
2000, and to be sure some changes (like ISO
9001-2008) have happened over the intervening years, but
nothing until the last few that would require a re-thinking
of some of the Quality Assurance principals discussed
in the first little book. The current version, ISO 9001-
2015, which was brought "online" a few years ago added
enough differences to warrant updating the book. First,
ISO 9001-through 2008 was pinned to companies making
a physical product, the service area of business required a
somewhat tortured reading of the standard to be relevant.
Second, and in my mind most important, with ISO 9001-
2015, ISO became a way to manage risk. Risk to the
product, the company, and to the users of the product or
service. I've added these concepts to the text where I think
they are most relevant.

Ask a CEO, or the company owner, or senior staffer if
they believe in quality, and they will launch into a quality
sepal that would get Hitler past St. Peter and into heaven.
It's like asking a politician his or her stance on opiates;

they all have the same short answer, then bend your ear for fifteen minutes regarding their strong anti-drug stance. Many company leaders can talk a good quality talk, but they lose steam when it comes time to walk the quality walk.

This book is for them.

Other sincere, but problem-plagued quality victims are the owners of small and mid-sized companies who started the business from scratch and can perform every one of the fifty jobs their current workforce are doing. These people are nuts-and-bolts-types—smart, hardworking, and ready for growth…but…they can't understand why those working for them don't carry the same quality torch. "Why can I make it right, but the workers often drop the ball?"

These folks know its time for a more formal quality system but are understandably scared of what they see as a huge outlay to become ISO certified, or personally certified as a Six-Sigma Yellow, Green or Black belt, or to commit the investment required for creation of a viable QA branch, for small companies, even a Quality Assurance Director. Nothing in this book will keep that from eventually happening. These folks may have read some of the quality stuff out there and are, with some good reason, scared to take the plunge.

This book is written mostly for them.

So, okay then, this book is *not* for the big guys—the GMs, Fords, and GEs can afford degreed quality engineers and people certified in every quality-genera-black-belt-lean-Six-Sigma out there, and there are quite a few! My focus is on the company that started in a single bay of industrial row and now has its own building with forty to fifty employees. I present real-life examples of quality gone bad, quality gone good, and functional definitions. I give those in the middle of their growth a place to start.

Consider this book a way to calibrate the CEO, owner, or senior staffers' "quality BS meter." Not every company needs a full-fledged quality assurance section but hire a quality consultant and that may be what they tell you to implement.

By the way, one really good use of Quality consultants is to perform a "Gap Analysis" which is a thorough examination of what your company is doing and how to correct many of the impediments to a functioning, high Quality operation. The Gap Analysis is a good add on to this book, indeed one could use what is written in here to create and conduct a decent Gap Analysis. I've added an audit checklist in the back of the book which could assist in doing a "self-gap analysis."

As the company continues to grow, it will need a QA group, or at least a QA Manager, even if they wear more than one hat, but maybe not just now. At the end of this book, anyone can begin a quality program as complex or simple as the managers feel is needed—ISO, Total Quality Management (TQM), and Six-Sigma based (DIAMC) as needed later, if wanted and required.

Like training, CEOs and managers see quality as a budget item in which money and people can be traded and shifted to other areas as needed. My experience has shown that most quality people are smart, articulate, and capable of wearing many hats. The talent pool concentrated in quality is not lost on the senior management of a company, regardless of its size. I argue against the impulse to use those folks outside of quality, doing so only if the company's resources are so limited that it's the only way to implement a Quality Assurance program. If your QA people seem to have too much time on their hands, give them this book.

Many top managers see the quality section or branch as a red ink item. I don't think it is, and will spend some time in Chapter 10 discussing "recovering the cost of quality."

I included some of the principals put forth in the newest ISO version, 9001-2015 in this new 2019 re-write and update of my original book. As mentioned above, the term "risk" is used throughout the 2015 standard, and is something we, as CEO's and company owners, must address.

Starting in Chapter 1, I will spell out where the quality assurance section should be placed on the organizational chart. I will clearly separate quality control functions from the role of quality assurance. This distinction seems blurred in even the most structured training given to those entrepreneurs leading those smaller companies driving the American dream. It is certainly lost on owners of smaller companies who don't have a Harvard MBA after their title. Many times, I've been introduced to "my QA group" by the owner or manager, only to find out that they are doing nothing but QC work. Obviously, those in charge missed that week's lesson. Frankly, though, solid leadership and adherence to producing a high quality, profitable product has practically nothing to do with higher education.

One troubling aspect of trying to sell quality to fellow workers outside the QA section is the "special language" we use to explain our business. "Pareto," "fishbone diagrams," "Six-Sigma," "standard deviation" (sounds like that might be XXX rated), "scatter charts," "drill down," "pick the low hanging fruit," "DMAIC," "SIPOC," "affinity diagramming," "force field diagramming," "stakeholder analysis," "multi-voting," and on and on—all of these have their place inside quality, but seem to lose validity when expanded to the wider universe of a company. That last sentence will forever banish me to the outskirts of quality academia, but I'd rather be outside with the rest of the world, with my "stakeholders," than inside a quality fortress where the foreign QA language is spoken.

I will spend a little extra time on ISO in this re-write, mainly because anyone doing business with the government, or any company getting government money must be at least ISO compliant. Many companies realize that to be qualified to get the work, they must have the basics of a "Quality System" in place and documented. This is *ISO compliant*, even if not *ISO Certified*.

Six-Sigma, and it's skinny cousin—Lean Six-Sigma, TQM, and quality circles—or whatever the quality buzz words in vogue this week happen to be, all were or are a means to an end, all have some strong areas, but in my opinion and experience, all miss one or more important points. I have developed a simple, common sense approach to achieving quality. It's not completely mine, but I've selected the best QA approaches from the many companies I have worked with and for—either directly, or as a consultant, or have visited as an Inspector for the clients I work for. I also have included many quality failures and their stories.

In a troubled company, unfortunately, the folks in the quality group may well be the bearer of bad news. Most of the time, mid-level managers look around the office for a back exit when the secretary announces the QA people. It's true. A good quality-shop has the sour data before the cellophane goes on the package. They may have known before the product was assembled. Let's be real here, shall we? Mid-level managers don't want bad news, especially if they will take the hit.

If pressed as to which quality system I like best, I'll stay with principals of Dr. Edwards Deming. He had it right, and all the rest of the quality theorists lose something when attempting to improve on his simple, clearly stated fourteen quality principals. I'm not alone. His fourteen points are easy to understand and, as has been demonstrated thousands of times, are quite possible to implement. I'll try to be the go-between for where many companies are, and where the good doctor suggests we be.

Because, as mentioned above, businesses must be ISO Certified or at least ISO compliant, I'll also follow that outline as we go through the steps to be a high Quality, consistent and profitable operation. My first suggestion is, that if you and the company has done everything mandated in the ISO 9001-2015 standard, and do not wish to go through the expense of an ISO Certification, and the work you are bidding on says to be ISO Certified, bid anyway and say your company is ISO Compliant. Just be sure that a third party Vendor Qualification Audit will show this to be the case.

So, with all this in mind, let's dive into making the Quality Assurance portion of your business work for the bottom line!

CHAPTER 1

TOP MANAGEMENT AND QUALITY

Problem #1—The CEO or Owner's position on quality is unclear.

Where's the beef?

ONE OF THE BEST AND MOST QUOTED COMMERCIALS of all time was the one done by the Wendy's hamburger chain, in which a couple of elderly women bought a burger and when one looked inside the bun exclaimed, "Where's the beef?" If the "beef" of a company is the CEO or owner (throughout this book, these will be synonymous), they are ultimately responsible and accountable for the company's quality, and in many companies, the "beef" question is valid. If they are the owner, then the viability of the business rests squarely on their shoulders.

A standard joke about a CEO in one of the companies I worked was that he was like the Easter Bunny—both were alleged to come out of hiding once a year. Actually, I had better luck seeing the Easter Bunny. Yet this CEO had his name on the quality policy. I can only assume that for the few seconds he looked at the document, he supported quality. The rest of the time? Who can say?

Several times I've written a company Quality Assurance manual for clients. In one case they had one, but it was 314 pages that no one read, and was impossible to follow. Mine ended up 28 pages. It was also not acted upon because the implementing of the manual was "going to be difficult." Yes, a company of 2,500 people couldn't see fit to have a Quality Manager and 4 Quality Officers. That particular Transportation Company will do *anything* for safety and quality, just so long as is doesn't require effort, people, and doesn't cost anything.

I don't mean to say the owner or CEO needs to be on the plant floor once a day with a big QA stitched in red letters on a baseball cap. The people doing the hands-on work do not need to see the CEO's up-close and personal support of quality. They have other reasons to build in quality—like good work instructions or in process-hold-point QC inspections. Most front-line people do not feel qualified, empowered, or responsible for continuous quality improvement—they should, but more on that subject later. Front line workers should see the CEO's quality plans through the actions of their direct supervisors and all above them with whom they interact. That said, by the way, seeing the CEO once in a while doesn't hurt!

Think about it. How much time, effort, and money does it take to have a semi-yearly, all-manager and supervisor meeting, in which the owner or CEO introduces the Director of Quality? All he has to do is point to this person and announce that this person is working directly for him and speaks for him in matters of quality improvement and quality policy.

Okay, this brings us to a logical place to mention the Organization Chart. ISO and most Federal Quality Assurance Guidelines (yes, the Feds have them!) insist on an up-to-date Org Chart in order to be considered for an award of a contract. This chart should have Quality Assurance as a direct report to the top of the company, and never to the manufacturing people, or to the engineering folks. That's right folks, the Director of Manufacturing cannot also be the QA manager. Nor can the janitor, unless he has the keys to the Exec-washroom…wait, he already does, doesn't he…OK maybe the janitor, but understand when the Quality Manager is acting in their role as such, they are equal to whom-ever they are working with, even the VP of sales, or the Director of Finance. The org. chart Quality Control block should be a dotted line through the QA, but may be a direct report to manufacturing if so desired. More on that later in the book.

There is no doubt in my mind that the people who need to see and hear from the highest level of the company that Quality Assurance WILL happen are the superintendents, their assistants, the foremen, and the supervisors.

If they do not understand that a company, even one that does well, must move toward continuous quality improvement (CQI), and that they are the ones to make it happen, they are just treading water, waiting for others in their business, their competitors, to throw them a cast iron life ring.

The support of quality by other people in the business is essential. I started with a discussion of the CEOs because they get the ball rolling, but they need those under them to keep it moving or it stops quickly. If those under the CEO are the starters of quality implementation, it can succeed, but finding senior staff willing to take initiative, get the budget for the money, fight for employee positions, empower a QA staff, and get them trained and started with a solid block on the org chart *without the CEO's "buy in" is unlikely.* This is another reason ISO and other quality plans and books start the process with the top manager, or CEO.

My skepticism of ISO being a meaningful way to assure quality going out the door does not diminish the fact that the committee of folks who came up with the ISO scheme years ago and re-furbished the plan for ISO 2000, then 2005, and 2008 were brilliant, and the newest version ISO 9001-2015 added even more relevant considerations to successful business. Several significant changes came about in the ISO 2015 discussions and during the extensive comment period, but one thing remained as step 1-Top management must sign on to quality, and they must be present, visibly and on paper. A good QA section can make money for any company. If a company loses money in spite of an active, qualified QA group, the QA people can tell the board exactly where the money was lost. They know where the bottlenecks are, where dinosaurs are blocking progress, and where the company is in comparison to the rest of the industry. Not only that, but good metrics and benchmarking of the industry, in which they operate will give business planning committees good data that senior management needs and wants.

All this said, I think I know why some CEOs shy away from placing the QA group properly in the company. *This portion of the discussion is directed towards those hired to run a company and does not apply to an owner unless they have just purchased an ongoing business.* I've identified three main reasons a newcomer may choose not to enter the quality game straight out of the box:

1. The CEO inherited a dysfunctional QA branch that can't properly communicate and implement the quality message. Restructuring and replacement of problem people is difficult, may be guarded by potential lawsuits, work, or union contracts, and just ain't worth it, so it goes on the back burner for at least several months after a CEO gets the exec. washroom keys and moves the pictures of the kids and dog to the new mahogany desk. He or she doesn't want an idiot sitting next door, even if the idiot is the inherited Quality Director.

   One QA manager I worked for spouted quality theory, but never was able to tie the theory into front-line operations. God bless her; she was one of the motivations for this book. Data collection went on forever, with the end report supporting the theories, but not the product and service. It was as if the entire QA branch was collecting data for her term paper. We later learned she was, at the time, in a Six–Sigma certificate program where the professors had never actually been in business or needed to make a quality group work. Did she have the CEO's ear? Doubt if he had her extension anywhere in his office.

Another believed QA personnel should be "in the trenches," inspecting continuously, visible to the workforce. While I agree with Quality Officers being visible, inspection is a poor use of a QA person's time. If a CEO knows anything about Quality Assurance, they would leave **that** QA manager out of the loop. Why put inspectors in the decision making chain? Inspectors are not the thinkers.

Yet another investigated a quality issue to death, producing a bale of paper with the entire history of the offending component and a fourteen-page executive summary! Who can blame a CEO for keeping such basket case managers at arm's length? Add gender and/or a minority status to the mix, and these losers become as untouchable as plutonium pellets. Many of these folks can point to past years' glowing performance reviews by people who couldn't tell the difference between QA processes and QC inspection. In the wage board's hearing, the incompetent QA manager can argue, "I was great for years. See the yearly reviews? How can I now suddenly be incompetent?" Well duh, the simple truth is they can't, they were always incompetent, and since the previous reviews were done poorly, they, therefore are untouchable.

2. The CEO joined the company with power structures firmly in place, systems that realized that having control over the budget, personnel, and direction of the QA branch was a way to move their contract, product line, or service force along _without proper quality oversight_. Most CEOs and a good number

of owners I've met are good at picking the hills on which they want to fight; that's how they got where they are, and why they can count on staying there. Wresting a slice of perceived power from long-established company structures for no clear and present gain ain't gonna happen.

I worked for a company where the QA branch was budgeted under and controlled by the engineering section. This section also controlled the procurement process and the capital improvement budget. Whenever a vendor's quality assessment audit or a process audit showed problems (sometimes well into the procurement) the documents were quashed. Soon, QA people were seen as impediments to the contract moving forward. At the same time, the QA director roamed the halls, looking for "low-hanging fruit," her office walls covered in fishbone diagrams of, well—as far as I could tell—fish. With so much QA newspeak, no one could take her, or the QA branch, seriously. The new CEO was convinced that the QA branch should stay where it was—out of his hair.

The procurements, without any Quality input allowed, were disasters. The theory and esoteric QA psycho-babble somehow didn't transfer to a complex quality system's oversight. The transit cars purchased under this regime, even though the newest in the fleet, are the ones slated for the first replacement when newer cars were ordered. The shiny finish covered poor engineering, bad designs, and shoddy wiring, all rendering the fleet out of service more than running making money for the Authority. By the way, all of which was documented by the QA officers, and ignored by the Program Management engineers.

Never forget that many upper-level managers understand that control of a budget should be protected. Money and positions in any sized company represent power. This control will be defended to the death—of the company. That decision cost the company millions and eventually was a big part of what led to the CEO at the time's release.

3. The CEO, and here perhaps the owner, has never been convinced that a well-run QA branch pays for itself many times over. As mentioned in the preface, everyone talks the quality talk, but walking the proper quality walk is more problematic. How many of us have seen re-shuffling of the corporate dominoes at every CEO change—you know, a new slogan, new consultants, the org chart with all new department names, and of course, new faces imported from wherever the CEO came from? In my experience, there has never been a meaningful or productive change in the QA section during these re-shuffling exercises.

Before we go too far in trashing new ways of doing things—you know, "thinking out–side the box" or "consider the customer family," or whatever the hell will fit on a reinvention poster—understand that America loves this stuff. The quality business is no different. In order for the large quality businesses to stay relevant, a new quality philosophy must be rolled out every decade or so. TQM, Quality Circles, ISO, Six-Sigma, and on and on. One could argue that the ISO 9001–2015 transition process fits that dynamic, as does the new improved "Lean Six-Sigma," again all have good points, and all have weaknesses.

To expand on #3 above, much of the American scene gets this reinvention; consider the re-writing of history, math, and English textbooks every six or so years. Just sell the "latest research on learning," and all the old books (serviceable for years to come) are relegated to the intellectual tar pit of extinction. And who can argue with the new fashions, many that leave your belly cold and your feet hurting? Yeah, buddy; new is better. But I digress.

I'll bet any reading this can talk of managers they could not get to move off the dime for quality or anything else.

Years ago, I worked as a signal and communications inspector for a small, profitable railroad on the east coast. A number of wayside telephones needed to be installed on a new section of track. The phones were mounted to switch ties—creosoted, ten-foot-long, 9"x10" blocks of wood. I saw in a railroad catalog that a company was making poles out of aluminum and ordered a dozen. The metal poles could be installed by one person, lasted forever, and were stronger than the ties after a few years in the weather. When they arrived, my boss said, "We don't use aluminum poles," and threw them over the hill into the woods behind the building. "We always use ties."

This same man had twelve men digging a ditch for signal wiring to a new signal location at a crossover being upgraded. He actually called in a construction worker to move a backhoe that was in the way of the ditch! The back-hoe construction guy offered to dig the ditch since he had a four–hour overtime minimum and was told "we always dig by hand." Lord, save us from dinosaurs.

Rumors of a comet wiping dinosaurs out are overstated. The dinosaurs we work with are a reality. Unfortunately, they are widely distributed throughout any established company. The most troublesome, in my experience, are those found in the upper management structure, and they are there to stay. They have been with the company the longest and have moved upward by the force of seniority. Dinosaurs promote fellow dinos. Dinosaurs may be also found around the owners of small to mid-size companies.

They are too low to get under, too wide to go around, then climbing over them gets you into the spikes on their backs, and some are carnivorous! They have a mantra— "Hey! Don't rock the boat."

Over time, don't we all get into "comfort zones" that are not good for us personally, and not good for our companies? Dinosaurs epitomize this. Be wary of change for change's sake, but fear of change is worse. Resident dinosaurs must be either convinced there's a better way or ignored as progress happens around them. If they do not believe that continuous quality improvement (CQI) is essential to stay in the black and spread success across the company, we are obligated to try to do it anyway. I'm not crazy enough to say we are never beaten down. Many of us have better hills to die on than in battle with a relic. However, we have to keep trying.

Several times in the past few years, I've run into the top guy in a smaller company who just won't move toward obvious and inexpensive ways of CQI for their company.

In the winter of 2014, I offered a suggestion to a company making castings for a client. The holes were off in what I felt was cumulative error, and the casting had warped because of a process that de-stressed it on one side. I'm not an engineer, but play one at the Christmas party sometimes, so I first suggested making all the holes as measured from the center one; that way, any possible error to the ends would be cut in half.

The destressing problem was a little more time consuming, but not a costly fix—just bead-blast the other side of the casting, de-stressing that side as well—self-straightening, if you will. Hell, consider it paint prep. If you don't know what bead blasting and de-stressing are, don't worry. They are simple manufacturing processes. The owner thanked me, but said they had always done it his way.

After a few months of their customer's source inspectors rejecting poor product and dealing with the resulting delays in shipments, they lost the contract. Less than $.50 per casting in additional labor, and just a little thought toward quality for items that would be sold for $380.00 each would have saved it. $7,752,000 net and about 1/3 of that profit down the tubes because the comet didn't get all the dinosaurs. In this little casting company, the owner had a glowing certificate with a flowery quality policy he had signed, so "Where's the beef?"

As far as the top manager is concerned, I'm amazed that a company cannot set aside two half-day slices of the work year to focus exclusively on the thing that can bury competition, make fat bottom lines, limit or eliminate complaints and lawsuits, and get a company recognized as the best—quality. I'm also amazed that all areas of change and movement are on the table when a new person shows up—except quality.

The Nutshell

- The quality message must start with those at the top of the company.

- There is no adequate way for a quality assurance section to work if top management does not *visibly*, as well as *philosophically*, support quality.

- The only way middle management can be properly motivated to take the quality message to the workers (empowering them to make quality happen in their work) is for top management to be seen supporting quality on more than a poster in the lunchroom.

- To whatever extent possible, the quality section should push for at least 2½ days a year of the top managers' time devoted to re-enforcing the quality message, in person and on stage.

- Quality people must be vocal advocates of their craft, even if those at the top of the company do not give proper support.

CHAPTER **2**

CAN ANYONE DIRECT ME TO THE QUALITY ASSURANCE SECTION?

Problem # 2—The reporting position of the quality group is misplaced.

Where is quality in the business structure?

THIS IS WHERE WE TALK ABOUT THE POSITION of quality in the organization. As a quality professional, I, of course, think it should be in an office adjoining the CEO or owner's suite, requiring the procurement, manufacturing, and operations people to pass a phalanx of QA officers armed with Tazer guns, pick through a minefield, and crawl a hundred yards in the mud under a thicket of rusty barbed wire infested with killer-bees before entering the boss's office. For this discussion, however, I suppose moderation of that position is desirable.

In Problem #1, we explored potential reasons for the QA branch being misplaced and that misplacement at least for the time being agreed to by the CEO or owner. I have worked for and observed companies where quality assurance reported to everyone from the production superintendent to the program manager of a big procurement. The worst was under a deputy general manager—a real nut case on a Saddam Hussein power trip, except Hussein may, if dissected by a team of cannibals, have had some good points, or points that tasted good.

I have yet to work for a company of any size where the QA people were where they should be, but I've visited a few. My personal Hussein was promoted from the engineering branch, therefore the QA group stayed there in engineering, even after he left.

If there is no way to convince the CEO and his staff to have the quality group as an org-chart solid line connection to his office (that's been my experience, and I trust it is a valid cross section of most quality shops), then I submit that the quality assurance people should be directly under the auditor general. They should be considered auditors, as that quality function produces the best and clearest "snapshot" of the health of the company's various quality programs. If no solid line org-chart is forthcoming, at least a dotted line needs to go into the CEO's office.

This is not to say that there is no quality function in procurement or manufacturing areas. They need some of their resources set aside for QC. The direction of this QC effort should be guided by documentation and reporting policies signed off on and distributed by the QA branch. In no case should the QA and QC people be the same, and in no case should the QA people work for those responsible for the goods or services the company is tasked to deliver. QC needs to be separate as well, but can be budgeted under manufacturing or procurement control. Manufacturing managers who have an understanding of quality can best set the proper human resources for the QC effort. The procurement people have often, in my experience missed a great opportunity to effect quality in a huge way. A more detailed definition of QA and QC is a little later in the book.

Many small businesses don't have a "procurement branch" as such, the owner of their shop or their fore-people do the ordering. But, if this is the case then they can also make that huge Quality leap. We'll discuss the purchase order as an often-overlooked place for Quality to start later in this book, but let's talk a minute about Source Inspections, and its close cousin Incoming Inspection. If an item is so important that your business will stop if it arrives at your facility and can't be used, should you not assure its correct when it left the factory?

If an item is important, but only ordered once a year because the people you order from only make them once a year, (specialty rubber products come to mind) should you not assure they are correct when they arrive at your shop? I have seen that often they go to the shelves, and are found to be defective later, long after the invoice has been paid! Now try to get the $$ back 6 months later.

It is human nature to pressure QA to back off if delivery schedules and late penalties, or liquidated damages, are on the table. I have been in meetings in which program management told QA reps that they were being "obstructionist" when their audits showed massive, undocumented, or clearly pencil-whipped inspection and testing of multi-million dollar vehicles. The actual statement was "I guess you quality people want us to just pack up and not take any more deliveries."

Noise and smoke; nonetheless, they avoided any meaningful discussion of the audit findings.

The story didn't end with one idiot's irrelevant commentary. Because the QA people worked under the engineering branch, which was also over the PM, the PM won—sort of. The vehicles didn't work, and the contract ran three years over! Modifications were still ongoing five years later, and not one of the performance goals was ever met! The chief engineer has been replaced—again.

Learned a lesson? I don't think so. At this writing, the same company is well into another procurement disaster of apocalyptic proportions. The CEO has been fired and will be leaving as soon as he can load the golden parachute money into the Escalade.

Early in my quality career, I was sent to a company that had made a run of 1,600 valves for the air braking system of train cars. This small company was the first place I saw clear evidence of pressure applied to quality for the sake of production. The quality group, actually a QC operation, had tested 100% of the valves. My company's young engineer who drafted the specification did not include environmental testing as part of the qualification. The valves had to be tested in service! They all worked, but when exposed to the first winter's blast of arctic air, a portion of the production run stuck closed, and the train wouldn't move. While we can all agree this is better than sticking open and the train not stopping, it's still a problem. Not all the valves were bad, but there was no way to separate them from the good ones, and worse, there was no unique serial number on a valve. All 1,600 had to be re-manufactured. The QC people had accurate records of how many were done on a particular day, but no numbers tying the valve to a test, and they worked for production. Production pressures kept them going out the door as soon as they were completed.

The actual mechanism in Quality for the above problem is called "containment" and will be discussed again a few times later.

Production must be insulated from quality in every possible way. Tracing even a day's run of valves would have saved that little company's bottom line for that year. One minute per valve, $.01 worth of ink and an Excel file with serial numbers, and this little company would have had another chance at making more air valves for the multi-billion-dollar transit industry. So close, but so far.

Most QA people take no pleasure in "I told you so." The customer or our company takes the hit, and the credibility of the company suffers. Suggesting another head count of the Indians to Custer would not have made the day for the cavalry any better. Watching the customers leave in droves is a sick feeling, and like Custer, seeing a mistake too late helps no one.

By ISO, and all high-thinking quality programs, the QA branch needs to be autonomous. Its budget must be separate from production and service areas, and not easily manipulated by internal company politics. That's why I suggest attachment to the CEO administration or the Auditor General's section. If the company does not have an Auditor General, QA should be under the accounting branch, or in a small operation, report directly to the owner.

They have the best chance of stemming unnecessary losses. Those sections normally have a good ear for the politics inherent in any company, and can direct QA function where the best bang for the audit buck can be realized. If we're talking about a really small shop, the Quality Manager should be right there with the owner, and the accountant.

Parenthetically, if the direct report person for the QA branch is in another state or country, even better. Less pressure from the locals is always a good thing.

The Nutshell

- The best position, from a functional and practical stance, for the quality assurance section to be is in the CEO or owner's administrative area.

- Failing a solid-line connection to the top person, the next best administrative position is under the auditor general or the accounting group, both from a managerial and budgetary standpoint.

- The quality section should never be budgeted under engineering, service, or production.

- The quality assurance section must be autonomous.

- Given clear instructions and supervision, it's good to have the quality section report to those away from production and service—maybe in another state.

- If an item is so important that your business will stop if it arrives at your facility and can't be used, assure its correct when it left the factory by a Pre-shipment Inspection.

CHAPTER 3

WHOSE QUALITY IS IT, ANYWAY?

Problem # 3—Assuming the level of Quality.

We will meet or exceed…Ya-da, ya-da, ya-da

AN INSTRUCTOR OF MINE ONCE WORKED FOR A cardboard supplier who got a big order to make boxes for books. The customer specified a weight of cardboard and gave the size of the book. The marketing people wanted repeat business, so they upped the strength of the cardboard and gave the customer a better box—on time and within budget. Several weeks later, a bill came in from the book people for $11,000—and a note from their attorney saying, "Pay up or lose in court." The extra weight of the upgraded cardboard had slipped the cost of mailing the books into another postal rate! The Book of The Month people knew exactly what they wanted, and clearly had it on the PO.

The customer sets the level of quality—always. Quality pledges that say, "We will meet or exceed the quality requirements of our customers" seldom do, and usually costs money. Good quality sells and gets repeat business, but the best #2 wooden pencil still ends up mostly as shavings in a sharpener someplace, and smart repeat customers will not spend extra money for something that does not add to the function of the product or its sale-ability.

That said, business people need to be sure that the customers are aware of what they are buying, what the level of quality is, and how it affects the cost. A good marketing group can get a higher price for quality if the customers do not know what they want and are properly educated on the benefits of the higher Quality. But if the customers are on top of their request and the specifications are clear, it's always the best business decision to give them what they ask for.

A top computer company ordered a million one-watt 5% 12K Ω film resistors from a large Japanese electronics supplier. They stipulated no more than three bad resistors in the order (Six-Sigma). The order came in with an envelope taped to the outside near the packing slip. Inside were three resistors and a note that read, "We don't know why you ordered three bad ones, but for your convenience, here they are."

While amusing, it illustrates the point. If you want a specific level of quality from that resistor manufacturer, that's what you'll get. Including those bad resistors was a good business decision!

The level of quality is second nature to most of us. We know that the best $19.99 TV steak knife is worth less than $19.99. No one made it at a loss, and some–body paid for the TV airtime. We know the over-stimulated, easily awe-struck, and way-too-happy idiot host, who is dazzled nearly to orgasm by the knife wielding, tomato, onion, and zucchini-savaging guy in a chef's hat at least got scale pay for the performance. If I ever decide to use a knife to saw a nail in half, perhaps I'll buy one.

When the knife (with a lifetime guarantee, if you send it back to eas tirmo reprodu ctssomepl aceint hearctic with $27.00 postage and handling) shreds a tomato after three weeks in the kitchen, we laugh and say, "Should have used it on a nail." Are we surprised? Twenty bucks for the best 137 knives in the universe? Come on. So, where is the best place for the level of quality to be spelled out?

ISO leans heavily on the purchasing documents, or the purchase order as the ruling document. Good purchasing departments eliminate big problems by getting clear expectations and specifications inserted in the PO. Businesses who take the time to have this clarity in the PO are in the best position if something goes wrong and later needs changing. Purchase orders have advantages over a formal contract in that they can be modified order-to-order and in some cases, in the middle of an order. Extra costs and new bids may be required, but doesn't that work to everyone's favor?

ISO registration and an ISO-based audit put weight on the PO and the receiving department. In my view, this is the second-best part of an ISO program. Dr. Deming points out that the lowest-cost bidder may not be the best. Assuring the vendor can deliver the product on time and to specification is worth a hell of a lot more than missed production schedules and lost end-customer business, even if the always-late company bids less than the always-on-time folk. This has been my experience—how about yours? Some of the best spent money on Quality Consultants is for **Vendor Qualification Auditing**. Having a neutral third party say that a company can't assure the quality of their product saves countless dollars later.

Even if a company can supply Quality, can they meet the demands? Predicating order fulfillment on having the workers work 12-hour days (even if they are well paid) is a poor model to become tied to for *YOUR* production. Studies show that after a few weeks' workers will slack off when on overtime, add hot Summer of cold Winter and take another 10% off production to standard. Quality suffers and this company should not get the work.

It is impossible to build a high quality product without quality materials. Incoming or source (pre-shipment inspections) are the lions at the gate for the quality our manufacturing or service people deliver. In order to reject incoming materials, however, the receiving QC people need clear guidance and training. A well–formulated PO is a start. Another good practice is to take every one of the supply people for a few hours on the line. Showing the parts clerks where the parts are actually used pays for itself hundreds of times over. I guarantee this day in the career life of a supply person saves big money for years to come.

I was told once by a parts guy, "I don't issue repair parts; I issue numbers." He was lucky, because if I had been the king, I would have fired him on the spot—maybe had him beheaded. Years ago, I was cruising an area where the company stored items to be surplused. I saw an entire pallet of new, in-the-box Timken® roller bearings—hundreds of them—waiting to go to the scrap dealer. These were big ones, specially made to our company's specification, and all certified. $125,000, ready to go to the scrap man for $0.11 a pound. They had been returned from a bus garage where they had been stored for years as "steering arms," and I had railcars out of service, awaiting bearings! Because no one in the bus garage could make the "steering arms" –AKA Timken® roller bearings work on a bus, the system showed no usage, so the part was deleted, and the bearings went to surplus. No steering arms for a long damned time, either, and now not even a part number for them! All the while, trains were out of service because of no bearings! Yes, those parts guys just issued numbers, certainly not common sense. I can write another book on dumb-ass parts department decisions, but it would be so over the top, though completely true, that it would not be in with business books; it'd be with Dave Barry in the humor section.

I will have a section on QC when we talk about inspection in Chapter 7, but some comments can be made here. Profits can be made if good engineering is combined with proper QC. As an example, if the engineering drawing calls for the holes in the base plate of a coffee maker that will wholesale for $13.00 to be .025" on 1" centers + -.0005, and QC is rejecting those out of that tolerance, a few things should happen.

> *The engineer should be fired*
>
> *His supervisor should be severely reprimanded*
>
> *The QA group should be put into the loop at an earlier point in the manufacturing process.*
>
> *The QC group should send up flares and wave flags*

The guys making the base plates should have a way to be heard (it's a guarantee they knew the problem)

BECAUSE

The tolerance makes no sense.

The hole should be bigger, and a pan head screw specified, so more base plates can be accepted and all of them can be made faster.

As soon as some were rejected, QA, QC and engineering needed to sit down and get it right.

To be competitive, realistic quality standards need to be in place. It costs an exponential of X2 to take a tolerance from .1 to .01 and X10 from .01 to .001, and God knows how much for .001 to .0001. My son, a good machinist, used to manufacture parts for NASA and DOD. He's convinced that excessively tight tolerances, while producing astounding quality, add to excessive unit costs with no functional gain.

Another point is that everyone in the manufacturing loop should be tasked and empowered to suggest ways to reduce the quality of a specific while not affecting the overall quality of the whole, to the betterment of the bottom line.

Most workers hired to build America did not walk off a space ship…well, maybe a few, actually maybe I've met some, but not most. They had varying degrees of experience in what our businesses do—you know, the neo-human-resources "skill set" thing. Most can tell you about bad management costing money, sometimes the company's existence, and that may be why we got the chance to hire them. Isn't it worth the time to ask their advice? Shouldn't we, as managers, insist they be empowered to make what we do better?

I strongly believe the most loyal thing one of my employees can do for me and the company is to tell me when I'm screwing up! How many reading this feel they can go to their boss to stop a management train wreck? Open door policy? My ass. Poor managers sometimes think workers telling them something is wrong is a problem. Some think and have the mindset that "a squeaky wheel gets the grease one time, then it's assumed to be defective and replaced." I suppose it's the "no one can tell the emperor that he's naked."

I managed several shops within a big transportation company. My MO for the first week was just to observe and make notes. The second was to sit down in neutral space, like the cafeteria, with every worker I supervised. I took all the time I, and they, needed to understand each other. I even built a profile of their expertise and hobbies. I found out one woman's hobby was photography, and I asked her to bring in some of her work. Her still life pictures showed me she had the equipment, lenses, and "skill set" to do close-up work. She was thrilled when I tasked her to photograph the acceptable and minimum acceptable standards, and later the in-process steps of complicated relay adjustments. This project grew shop-wide as we all became involved with establishing and documenting best practices. We all learned, and by the nature of the project, became a team.

From the data I collected (more on that later), our re-built materials and components worked better than new, and it was due to the empowerment of the workers, not my brilliance. The workers wanted to do a good job and were allowed to do so. We succeeded in spite of poor management several levels above us. Empowered, quality-savvy workers can drag some heavy anchors and still get the ship to port. Quality, when allowed to happen with a little guidance, normally will.

The Nutshell

- It is always the best business decision to allow the customers to set the level of quality.

- Efforts to exceed the customer's specified level of quality can be costly with no gain in customer loyalty or market share. Streamlining processes can advance CQI, even when there is no actual increase in the quality of the product.

- Empowerment of the workforce to produce new ideas as well as improvement in process is the most practical way to achieve CQI and everyday quality.

- Poor management is not an excuse for not working toward CQI and better bottom lines. This effort toward our success, our "selfishness," is a true win-win.

- All specification tolerances, special work requirements and operations add cost, this cost should always be weighed against any possible improvement in Quality. Is it worth it?

CHAPTER 4

QA–QC IT'S ALL THE SAME AND IT'S ALL A PAIN

Problem # 4—Those who should know the difference in QA and QC don't.

Drawing the distinction between QA and QC

I T SADDENS ME TO CONFESS THAT THE TITLE of this chapter was an actual statement made to the quality assurance group I worked in as a quality officer by a new manager who thought he was being glib. He wasn't, and the statement was as out of place as a sexist blonde joke in a N.O.W. convention hall elevator.

Here's the quick and dirty definition:

> **Quality Control is concerned with the end quality of a widget.**
>
> **Quality Assurance is concerned with the ability of all widgets to meet a specified quality standard.**

We use this definition throughout this book, although the real definition is somewhat longer. It seems many in quality just can't use ten words when three thousand will do.

As mentioned before in Chapter 2, there is a quality function in the procurement and manufacturing areas. They need some of their resources set aside for QC. Quality Assurance should be responsible for the direction of this QC effort. The QC people should be guided by documentation, and reporting policies signed off and distributed by the QA branch.

In no case should the QA and QC people be the same, and in no case should the QA people work for those responsible for the goods or services the company is tasked in delivering. Yes, I said it again, maybe will a few more times by the end of the book!

QC needs to be separate as well, but can properly be budgeted under manufacturing or procurement control. Manufacturing managers who have a proper understanding of quality can best set the proper human resources for the QC effort.

Quality Assurance

In discussing what QA does, let me give an example. I have attended many FAIs, or first article inspections, as a quality representative. Normally, engineering people examine the thing to see if it's made to the specification, if the color is right, if it weighs what it should, and if it works. Maybe a test procedure is examined.

As the QA representative at the FAI, I peel off as soon as I can and go the manufacturers QA section. I'm not concerned that a major manufacturing facility is able to make one of something (I can do that in my shop at home). I want to see if a process is in place that can make 10,000 items and hold the quality to the FAI piece's standard, using a repeatable, easily understood, clear (with diagrams), and processes available to the workers—a process with QC inspection points and written check-offs for them.

The process used must be in the language of those using it. If a majority of the workforce is French, the process should be in French as well, even if, like most French people I've worked with, they tell you they don't need a process – that's a joke…sort of. There should also be an English version if those tasked with inspecting and auditing are English speaking. An effort should be made to assure special words that do not directly translate are adjusted to have the meaning intended.

Nothing builds in repeatable quality better than a good process.

The lack of a clear and up-to-date process for whatever the task is at hand, is one of the risk points highlighted in ISO 9001-2015. The risk even goes into areas within the process. I've worked on mechanical units where the security of the hardware is crucial, but there are no torque amounts spelled out, not tightness witness marks required, and no certified torque wrenches in the facility! Now, there's risk front and center.

Everybody concerned, workers, engineers, managers and QC people need to develop processes for the slice of the manufacturing or service pie they are tasked with accomplishing. If quality issues develop, going to the process is the best way to have a long term addressing of the problem.

Quality Assurance should be responsible for assuring good processes. All of the processes need to have Revision (rev) levels and be signed by someone responsible for the process being followed. Within the company the processes should follow a uniform format, and be defined for the specific thing being built, inspected or tested. Any process documentation required to be completed during the process should be identified, defined, a sample provided, and what is to be done with the paperwork. Quality Control should be tasked with implementing these processes, as well as their initial development and updating. Note that ISO and in fact the courts have determined that a Quality created document, one created in the course of following a procedure, is a LEGAL PIECE OF PAPER, and saying on that paper that something was done, tested, or completed when it was not can be the grounds for legal actions.

Process development is not that difficult. Once a workable outline is in place and understood by those using it, adding new ones or modifying existing processes is simple. Bookstores are full of process guides, most likely even a Process Writing for Dummies, or The Complete

Idiot's Guide to Process Writing. When the auditors come-a-knockin' at the plant door and start asking those huddling inside why they did what they did, there is no better answer than "I followed the process, and here it is."

Most of the things we do in the manufacturing or service industry can be described in simple versions of everything else. Think outside the box on this one and see if that statement isn't true.

A few projects ago I was at a big-name electronics manufacturer conducting a source inspection, in the industry called a PSI – pre-shipment inspection, (QC for my client). I opened one of the communications units on the list and removed the cards so I could inspect the motherboard. I noticed one of the screws holding the motherboard to the frame was missing. When I pointed this out to the QA manager witnessing the pre-shipment inspection, his comment was "We put in thousands of screws; we're bound to miss one every now and then."

In a completely deadpan voice I said, "Okay, please show me assembly instructions indicating which and how many can be missed, and please disassemble this entire unit so I can be sure the missing screw isn't loose in the bottom of the unit someplace. Missing is one thing; loose in the bottom of the box full of electronics is another."

The ramifications of the QA guys statement are obvious, but it pissed me off so much that even now years later I think I'll go on about it for awhile. When we, the owner, manager, or QC lead person puts on the Quality hat, there is an implied obligation to the company, and our clients and customers. We, as Quality professionals have a responsibility to the notion of quality as a goal worth pursuing. Although I was ashamed of the QA manager's comment, I didn't show it – to him. I think we all have stories of a quality misstatement. I can only hope we can't give an example of our own anti-quality comments. Based on his comment, I now require a Non-Conforming Report (NCR) be opened for every discrepancy I find at that vendor. If the QA guy at the plant won't enforce quality, I will!

I'm not that much of a stuffed shirt, and I know some of the things we hear really are funny. I was looking at a batch of cables. They were terrible. Nicks and cuts in the wiring, incorrect length, no pull tests for the crimped pins for the run, and maybe more. As I kept adding to the reject pile, the young man assigned to bring the cables to me for inspection said, "If you think these are bad, you should have seen the ones we did last week!" The vendor eventually was disqualified, due in no small part to the evidence that they had an out-of-control process, which I proved with a process audit. I suggested the audit be done to my client, based on the comments of the worker, and the staggering number of failed cables. In that mid-sized cable manufacturer, the quality people spent all their time inspecting and having product repaired, and no time on improving the process. Beginning to see one of the places ISO 2015 defines the risk here?

As discussed before, Quality folk can wear many hats, but I suggest we be left to quality. A few I know were even used as a police force to beat up supervisors with audits and inspections if the Assistant General Manager in charge of the QA budget held someone in disfavor. The quality people quickly became intensely disliked, and it took years for the branch to get its credibility back.

Quality Control

As a consultant, I wear a QA hat sometimes, and sometimes a QC hat. I work hard to make sure the client is aware when the hat changes. It's not a billable hours thing; it's that I'm always trying to draw the distinction so others can learn the difference. For me, some of the QC work is far more interesting than the QA.

When my baseball cap has a big yellow QC on it, I get to see how stuff is done, and at least as rewarding, I meet those doing it. I've watched machines placing components on a circuit board so small you need a 10x loupe to see them, and the next week seen a sixteen-cylinder diesel engine taller than me and fifteen feet long being placed in the frame of a new locomotive. Inspection and QC can be interesting, even fun. Quality Control people provide assurance that processes are followed, documented, and that adequate data is collected for good quality metrics and product tractability. Remember the example of the little company making the air brake valves? With no traceability tying the valves to the test, and the dates of manufacture, even though the sticky grease problem was identified, which valves were effected could not be. All were then considered bad. Using the traceability to define problem units is called *"containment"* and can save thousands of dollars, and limit that pesky RISK. With proper, and by the way normally very inexpensive steps added to the process good traceability can be built into every item being built or repaired.

How about service folks? They can be part of the traceability thing too. In service, finding out who is not carrying the Quality ball at the clients location, or on the yearly inspections may be more important than minor issues in the factory. If I buy a $2,000,000 CAT scan machine that is out of service due to poor maintenance, it does me little good to have the supplier and the manufacturer in a circular firing-squad blame game. Now where's the risk?

Staff quality control people can also wear a number of hats. I've always felt QC people should have intimate knowledge of the task; perhaps the best are those promoted into QC from the production line. While some monkeys can be trained to do inspections, only the ones on TV can go back in and effect change in the process. Remember, as part of the entire quality picture QC also *must also work for CQI.* Those who just go back to the line and have the defect fixed without correcting the process have wasted time and money. They have identified a point of risk and left it in the process.

QC starts in the receiving department. If good stuff doesn't come through the factory door, it can't leave from the other end. Again, QC people need a handle on the process, but not the manufacturing process; this time it's procurement, the PO, and incoming inspection.

QC extends to the packaging and shipping areas on the other end of the plant. It does little good to make a perfect set of bar bells if they end up rolling around the delivery truck because the box disintegrated when it encounters the notorious Washington, D.C. streets. QC people are in the trenches, and should be the first line of communication when there's a problem, the first we seek out when we get to the plant floor with our audit materials in hand.

My quality assurance work (QA process audits or capacity audits) tends to be more tedious than QC work.

As an outside source inspector, I learn every day from the pre-shipment inspections I perform. That said, I have to admit it's rewarding to do an ISO bridge audit, a vendor qualification audit, or an ISO gap analysis, but it normally ain't as fun as talking to the people who really make stuff.

The Nutshell

- Many in business do not have a functional definition of the differences in quality assurance and quality control. We must draw that distinction and make it clear to those needing to know the difference.

- The QA and QC functions must be separate, both from their daily activities as well as where their budgets reside.

- QC people are the implementers of good, established process.

- QC people are the logical collectors of the data to be used to track quality metrics.

- QC people are responsible for creating, documenting, and implementing traceability.

- QA and QC can be critical in reducing risk to the company, our clients and customers.

- QC must be expanded to include incoming, and shipping departments.

- If QA is required to do QC work, or visa-versa, their respective budgets should take the monetary hits.

- All in quality, QA or QC, should be able to clearly draw the distinction between the two and communicate this distinction to others.

- Management should expect their QA and QC people to carry the flag for Quality and be defenders and even cheer-leaders for Process, and Risk management.

CHAPTER 5

WE DO IT BETTER THAN ANYONE ELSE, AND WHEN WE SCREW IT UP WE FIX IT BETTER, DON'T WE?

Problem # 5—Not benchmarking the business we are in, not collecting relevant data, and not fixing a quality problem correctly.

Bench marking

THEORETICAL QUESTION: IS BENCHMARKING CHEATING, LIKE STEALING CORPORATE data from competitors?

In most of the vendors and companies I have worked for and with, benchmarking is a hard sell. It's difficult for a manager tasked with doing it the best to spend money for a bunch of quality geeks to prove they aren't.

That said, if we can get out there and do research of our own industry, the results could be awesome. Some feel that processes are company secrets, and to be sure some are. I argue that special, proprietary processes are probably not the places where company "A" and company "B," doing the same thing in the same business, are different. Perhaps the chemical industry is an exception, but there aren't many others. Getting information on product flow or incoming inspection shouldn't be considered cheating.

Cheating is not a good way to describe benchmarking, but some less than upfront processes can be utilized to get information, if we are dealing with paranoid competitors who feel everything they do, did, or will do is a secret. One transportation business wouldn't give me schematics of a power supply that had been out of production for twenty-five years, and had no parts currently used by any power supply people! The schematic was "proprietary." Idiots. I had one come into the shop burnt up, how were the people in my repair shop supposed to re-wire it?

Below are a few ways to get information that can assist in setting a level to which our company should be producing.

One good way is to keep abreast of the state of the art in the various manufacturing machines and technology used in that business process. Sales people are more than willing to say you need a TS-3300XLT Laser Guided Ball Bearing Counter because your competitor just installed three on his line and now can count ball bearings eighteen times faster than you can. The people who make money keeping the latest equipment in front of potential customers should not be overlooked as a source of the latest advances. And remember, when quality improves in a type of product, everyone benefits.

We all know about trade shows, so I will only say that some of the best information I've gotten comes from the aisle conversations around the new equipment booths. Playing trade show cards a little close to the vest will garner tremendous information about the latest in the industry if we use the time-tested tactic of just listening.

Trade publications often give information about companies in articles. While most are fluff and only set out information the interviewed company wanted in the marketplace, consider these honest statements: "I read with interest the article on Fonebeam Rubber in *Liquid Latex Monthly* and was wondering to what you attribute your success?" When asked why you want this information, a truthful answer is, "I'm collecting information on the industry for a quality assurance program I'm trying to sell."

Never lie.

Always verify benchmarked information, and it's in the best interest of those in whatever industry to make the benchmark report available to anyone who wants it. Redact specific company information. Specific company information is not as important as the benchmarked data. What? Give away company secretes? Yes. Well, some, anyway. We all benefit in our industry if the perception of that industry is improved. Kind of the way raising the level in the pond makes it easier for all the boats in it to navigate.

A little benchmarking experiment: If you have a few weeks when you're not doing anything, get online and ask Google about anything—say, lemons—then go to all 3,384,963 places it lists and see if there is anything about lemons, bad cars, the 60s rock group, or the often confused cousin, the lime, that you don't know. The Internet is a good place to get benchmark data and to confirm data collected elsewhere. Remember that **free Internet information** might be the mother lode of data, but it could also be **worth what you paid for it NOTHING**. Verify!

Many of the businesses out here in flyover country are not in competition, even though they're doing the same thing. Public transit comes to mind, as well as any of the government activities. How about utilities, sewer and water, trash collection, and waste management?

Benchmarking can be direct and pleasant in these situations. Okay, maybe not benchmarking the sewage treatment operation of Podunk West Virginia, but most are not as olfactory challenging. What is the statistical likelihood that we, the South Podunk Power and Light Company, are doing everything the best in the country? Smart power companies are willing to share their ways of doing things and get data back from others. Those not willing to share probably can be studied, but not by us. Maybe not the archeological department of the local university—they're into dinosaurs and dying things.

Many of the benchmarking gurus say we should look for the best in the industry. Fine, but what if there isn't one? I mean, if company "S" is best at design, and company "N" at production, and plant "A" at customer service, and Canadian company "F" is the best at catalogue sales and "U" is the most solid in quality metrics, I submit the benchmark leader is the theoretical company called SNAFU.

Benchmarking a segment of an industry also serves to take a large project and allows us to break it into manageable pieces. In some cases, it also allows the quality workforce to focus on their best talents. Internal CQI? Perhaps. Breaking the benchmarking task down also allows us to get ideas on how to fix the most broken part of our company, then go on to smaller problems as we fine-tune the system.

It's always good to footnote and have several sources for benchmarked data. Nothing is worse than telling the senior staff that the company is near the bottom of the barrel for production, quality, and repeat business in the entire shoe snap and brass eyelet business, then having the CEO say, "Oh, yeah? Prove it," and not being able to.

Internal relevant data

Pity the poor NCR

Having the best benchmarking data in the world on our industry is worse than useless if we don't have anything to compare it to once inside the walnut-paneled walls of our "penthouse corner QA office suite." One of the first relevant places to begin our data quest might be to look at rejected materials, from either a sub-contractor or an internal manufacturing or assembly process, then go to the documentation of the rejection. Most of the companies I visit in my consulting business look at an NCR (non-conforming material report) much like a registered letter from the IRS auditing department, our dentist informing us of a needed root canal, or perhaps a phone call from the ex-wife's ball-busting attorney, probably bad news. I'd like to suggest here that this ain't necessarily so; at least, not most of the time. A good NCR system, called things like MRR (material rejection report) or MRB (material review board) or a SCAR (supplier corrective action request), which are all the same from a philosophical point of view, can really work to quality's advantage. I have always felt that a properly completed NCR can end a quality problem on the spot. Unfortunately, most NCRs are poorly done and as useless as teats on a steer as a quality tool.

Consider the "root cause" section of the NCR. I've seen countless NCRs that repeat the problem as the root cause. As an example: "defect = Bolt holding rocker will not tighten, threads in cam follower do not go to bottom of hole." And the root cause: "Threads do not go to bottom of hole in the cam follower, so rocker will not tighten."

In the root cause section, I'd like to see something like, "Procedure for threading cam follower was not specific in requiring a bottom tap to be used to assure the threads extend to the bottom of the hole," followed by the corrective action section being specific as to how this problem could be eliminated in the future. "The threading procedure, TP301-5, rev3, was changed to include the instruction 'bottom taps will be used after start and plug taps for all blind holes in cam followers.'"

Advocate everyone tasked with answering an NCR to take extra time in answering. I suggest going into more detail than is actually required. When writing an NCR, I like the addition of a specific time in which follow-up action will be taken. Resist the impulse to "make it go away." As a quality auditor and source inspector, if I'm the one auditing or inspecting an improperly done NCR, I am just like the mangy, worm-laden, flea-bitten cat that your daughter fed that cold November day seven years ago, which hates you, and barfs at your feet while you're eating breakfast with a hangover, I too, will not go away!

The notion of properly identifying root cause needs some more ink. A good company I'm familiar with called TapRoot® has a product line that makes the case that proper identification of root cause is the best way to prevent recurrence of nearly any problem. I agree. Incidentally, they give a good and informative seminar. Check 'em out at **www.Taproot.com.** Moving back down the line to the place a quality problem actually started is always best as we work to eliminate quality problems at the other end of the line.

One way to work to minimize risk in getting non-compliant product or service is to be careful to define NCR, MRR, and MTB procedures in the specification or purchase order if a specification is not part of the procurement in question, or the RFP, and finally the actual contract. Be clear that as the purchaser, you must have total veto power over repairs, use as is, or any modification or change in the spec. that would allow the questionable part to be shipped. Conversely, if we are the seller and want to maintain control over the entire spectrum of the manufacturing processes, we need to write the MRB procedure, keeping control within. If we get this power in the contract, it behooves us to be sure we don't pencil whip MRBs and can prove we have proceeded with due diligence.

On one project I worked, the MRB procedure was very specific. The manufacturer was the sole arbiter of the disposition of rejected materials. If a hole was drilled in the wrong place and a patch had to be done (no procedures for how to do the patch), there was no recourse for the customer! The vast majority of the rejected items fell into the "Use As Is" category, even though the engineer (if there was one) making the decision had never set eyes on the issue, and in fact was not even on the same continent as the problem!

The notion that customers were buying the thing new, not re-painted, scratched, repaired, dent-fixed, epoxied, or with a poorly done patch was lost on the manufacturer. Worse, we had no legal recourse for not accepting the "used, repaired, repainted, and welded" unit.

Researching returns and customer complaints should not be overlooked as we navigate the quality jungle looking for places to document our quality. This area should also be part of the thinking when doing benchmarking exercises. We all know the poison pill scenario, where someone got a bad product and forever tells everyone that the cell phone he got from Blab-Com didn't work, and no one was there to help get the thing working. It's not relevant that they never charged the battery, never took the cellophane off the mouthpiece, and never entered the activation code. Yes, many quality issues we deal with…aren't. Our job is not only to de-toxify the poison pill, but also to turn him from the dark side.

It is a powerful statement to hear on the phone, "I'm Bill Wheezer, the head of quality for Blab-Com, and I'd like to rectify your problems." Can I interject here that Bill does not have to be the head of quality? He is, however, the head of this quality issue, isn't he? The same effort should go into this customer that would be commanded by any other NCR. Obviously, this would not work for a large company or one with a lousy product, but they are not reading this, are they?

De-fusing a poison pill normally isn't that hard. All that's required is to take responsibility for what we own and be able to communicate what's not. One of my favorite radio talk show hosts recently said to a caller, "I'm really sorry, but based on your statement you are not intelligent enough to participate in this discussion. Thanks for listening, though, and please do not feel obligated to call again."

God in his wisdom has set limits on genius, but not on stupidity. I digress; the bottom line for poison pill neutralization is always the refund.

What about a real quality issue that some unfortunate customer has been inflicted with? Well, rather than see doom and gloom, how about seeing an opportunity for quality improvement? How's that for pounding a little sunshine? But think of it, producing a good root cause analysis of how this singular being came to this place in the time-stream of the cosmos, right in the midst of their carefully conceived plans, details, cell calls, and coordination, planning for the nearly the whole next hour— well, nearly a whole hour—only for the plan to crumble when they end up with a defective ribbon-bow making machine with Grandma's 104th birthday only three days away. Yes, their personal disaster can actually help our process. It's back to discovering the real problem, carefully documenting it, and getting the data back to the QC people who can fix the process so we can "okay" a close to our internal NCR.

I buy jukebox and pinball machine parts from a vendor in Chicago. Everything I get from them has damaged packaging and sometimes damage inside. This company is out of business and just doesn't know it yet. Every time I call them, I get the same answer. "Yeah, we know. I'll tell the shipping department to get it right. Can I send you another one?" I always say yes, and the next one comes in a tattered box, just like the last one. I could reduce their costs and improve their service over the phone. If we, here in this place, can see how to save money and improve the bottom line, why can't they? Couldn't any of us in the quality business help them out? The answer may be in the next chapter.

The Nutshell

- Quality resources must be made available for collection of benchmarking data.

- Benchmarking is the best way to keep abreast of industry advances that can be brought home for the betterment of the bottom line.

- Benchmark data collection is a good way to round out the knowledge base of quality and other staff.

- Internal data on the quality status of the company needs to be derived from sources other than other department reporting.

- Collected data must be concise and to the point.

- Non-conforming material reports can be an effective tool in driving quality back to its source.

- NCR, MRB, and other non-conforming data should be thoroughly investigated to drive quality back to the root cause of the problem for correction.

- We must keep quality control over the NCR, MRR, or MRB processes if we are to exercise proper quality assurance in defect resolution.

- Time should always be spent to investigate customer complaints, even those not our fault.

CHAPTER **6**

WHAT EXACTLY DO YOU QUALITY ASSURANCE PEOPLE DO, ANYWAY? CAN YOU HANG THIS PICTURE FOR ME?

Problem # 6—In your company, the quality assurance people...aren't.

QUALITY PEOPLE ARE NORMALLY ARTICULATE, SMART, AND CAN be paper trained in a few short months, if the lunch brakes are limited to two hours daily. This has led to my being tasked with correcting inept engineering, documenting federal guidelines for procurement, painting the office, investigating the cause of a wreck, auditing a class on sexual harassment, assembling cubicles, inspecting anything that moved, inspecting anything that didn't move, breathed, or didn't breath, and moving furniture. Did I mention correcting inept engineering? All fun, exciting, challenging, and stimulating character and career-building tasks to be sure, but marginally connected to QA at best, and at worst, not even a distant cousin twice removed.

The principal job of a QA section should be monitoring, documenting, and improving processes. Sure, other stuff like gathering quality metrics, performing quality-related audits, being an advocate for continuous quality improvement, assisting QC in their understanding of quality, while delivering sparkling political and social commentary can be thrown in. But mostly, we keep an eye on process. We discussed process earlier because it tied into the distinction between QA and QC. If we remember that good processes are critical in the path to minimizing risk, then that's time and QA money well spent.

Having the Quality Assurance people (or person if a small company) get involved with process, even before the item is being manufactured is also a proper use of QA. This is not to say the processes will be a finished product when we have a finished product...okay that was tedious phrasing. The process documents must always be considered a living document, changes and edits to streamline the process, maybe saving time and money, is another worthwhile use of QA resources.

So then, to make the necessary changes the main thrust of the process work the QA branch should be doing is collecting data on the way the processes are working—or not. This data collecting activity is loosely defined as gathering quality metrics. Please draw the distinction between what we discussed in the previous chapter and this data. What we want here is for the collection of data to show management where the company needs improvement, even if we're not doing too badly, if continuous quality improvement is to take place. You know—the digital snapshot of Grandma with the wart on her nose before we get out the software air-brush.

Before we were talking about correcting quality issues one at a time, and yes, hopefully this would expand into better processes. Here I want to explore making a better product without addressing a specific complaint.

There may a fight a-brewin' when we begin this task. The dinosaurs are lurking in the hall, ready to buttonhole the CEO with their sirens song: "If it ain't broke, don't fix it." If this were true, wouldn't we be all driving Ford Model A's?

Change for change's sake should be avoided, but there are ways to move CQI forward without falling into the "change is better" trap. What if quality can streamline a process so that, even if we don't improve the end quality, we raise the bottom line? I argue that qualifies as CQI and is effective in being a dinosaur repellant when presented to the owner or CEO.

If we found through data collection that many who buy or use our products are unhappy because they don't know how to use them, and if streamlined instructions with a shortcut card that gets them up and running quickly would add to the enjoyment of the product, I submit this also would be a quality improvement. Isn't anything that makes what our company does or sells better for the customer or the bottom line a good thing? Isn't that CQI?

We should take time to examine what data we are collecting and be critical of the time (money) it costs to collect this data. We must carefully determine the return that information gives us. It's true that some quality data must be collected and retained as quality records, and some (hopefully) will never be used, like test data we retain to protect the company in the event of a lawsuit down the road. In the case of the air valve company, proper quality documents would have saved their market for Transit air valves. That said, this discussion is of the data we collect just to document how our processes are working.

It's a hard sell to management to begin collection of data that will not be displayed on a chart for a year when analysis of the comparative data is available, but it must be done. Collecting relevant data ain't cheap. The folks filling in the forms are taking time away from their regular job. They may need training on the data collection, and they will need feedback if they are to be expected to stay on the page as the information collection process moves forward.

How many of us have access to "company history" or sometimes called "Corporate History"? I'm not talking about the three-ring binder in the reception area with the picture of the company softball team. I'm talking about documentation of attempts at CQI *that didn't work and why*. I worked for a company for twenty-five years and never saw a single historical document of value. The QA section is the logical place for company history to be documented. Countless dollars are spent repeating mistakes because the folks who made them the first time are retired, dead, or fired, and there is no record of their effort. Often, those making the mistake do not see it as a valuable learning experience, rather a SNAFU that needs to be covered up and forgotten.

Several articles in the past few decades have spoken to the astounding amounts of money and internal effort large companies waste by duplicating work. The Newark office is not aware that the Charlotte office is working on the same software update project, and may even be bidding against other offices in the same company! I worked for a company where this happened. The bidding war was fierce, and in the end, the two bidders left kept slashing the bid until the "winner" got the work, but lost their ass. Either division could have made money at the original price; one was an office on the East coast, the other an office of the same company in England! This is where I have to ask, "Are we in quality effectively demonstrating that we know what the hell we are doing, and maybe more importantly, communicating that to the throngs of the unwashed?"

Several ways quality people collect data and try to display it are just not effective. Consider a Pareto chart. To me, they all look the same. Indeed, if the Pareto principal is in force, they must look the same, and yes, I can pick the damned thing apart. From a quality theory standpoint, the dead bean-counting French guy has his place. I really think the Pareto principal should be a societal constant. Twenty percent of something will take eighty percent of the rest of it, be it money, sex, employees, food, or quality problems, but charting this by Pareto leaves a lot to be desired. Data needs to be put out there and easily understood. If everyone understands a Pareto diagram, then it is effective in showing where the problems are.

Another highly touted way to identify where process falls down is the scatter chart. Most scatter charts I have done or examined never show where the problem is like in the textbooks. All the ones I've done accurately showed a process way out of control! In-control quality processes will not be demonstrated well by a scatter diagram unless one is looking for true outliers, wild hair issues that are a pain but only happen a few times a year. They look like a well-choked twelve-gauge shotgun blast at twenty feet. Out of control processes rarely have only one cause. The shipping problems my jukebox parts vendor in Chicago has is an example of a business whose problems could be documented by a scatter chart, if that were the only problem they had.

The display of data should be pinned to the level of understanding that the audience possesses. The basic rule of communication is to broadcast, be received, and the transmission be understood. Pie charts, bar charts, line graphs with no more than three lines are examples of data displays well known by most people that can be produced in nearly any format. If senior management is in the meeting, use bright colors and cartoon figures... just kidding... sort of.

It takes time to collect good data, so good planning is needed to assure that all the data being sought means something after it's analyzed. We need to give those who give us the time and money for data collection reasonable expectations of what will come of the project.

This may not be as hard as you think. I recently commented to a new quality supervisor that the method of tracking the revision levels on their circuit boards was deficient. She said she was not able to get production or engineering to support a better system. I pointed out that they were in the process of bidding a job for aviation and would never pass a process audit by those in aviation, even if they were the lowest bidder. Traceability is important anywhere, but especially in avionics. With this in her argument, revision levels are now well documented on each circuit board and reflected in the complete assembly.

One QA shop I worked in had a very good guy who collected information every morning on train delays, their causes, and where the delay happened in the last twenty-four hours—all before eight a.m. His (our) boss wanted it in case her boss wanted it. In two years, the big boss never did. Later, I found out that the AGM had that data presented to him by operations in a streamlined report that took no time to compile since the operations people were inputting it as it happened throughout the day. Our analyst had to go into the computer files and re-copy their data for the QA report that, by the nature of its database, could not be more accurate than the one presented by rote and never requested. What a waste!

There are simple rules for the collection and display of data (QA Speak = Metrics).

Quality data (metrics) should seldom be derived from another internal operations source, unless it is used by QA as comparative data. Data for quality metrics needs to be collected in ways specific and relative to QA. Others can get their own data for their own purposes, and some can cross over, like time motion studies or FIFO (first in, first out) charting, and some others, but not many. When collecting quality data, I always remember that we are auditors, and as such, we need data that cannot be manipulated by those trying to show a better picture of their quality than may actually exist.

Detailed discussions of Quality metrics are a field in themselves and are outside the scope of this little book. It's been my experience that either QA sections don't have good data, or they have more useless crap than anyone can use or wants. There must be a happy medium, right? How many of us have been tasked to do a "quick and dirty" analysis of a costly problem because there wasn't time to derive metrics before the poopies hit the ventilator? How many of us were satisfied with the metric product we delivered, especially since it had, as its starting point, the time the problem was recognized?

The data presentation should be understandable by any wino under a bridge, in the dark, at thirty feet in the rain. Keep the principle simple. People who get lost in the data will not admit they are off the page, especially if they are supposed to be smarter than we are. They might be the ones needing to take action. Remember, for many, a promotion into management is accompanied by an immediate thirty-point increase in IQ and fifteen years additional experience, isn't it?

The data should have something to do with the problem or discussion at hand.

In an investigation of a derailment of a train, my QA manager wanted to know when the oil was changed in the air compressor. Most reading this probably don't know much about train derailments but can see that there is no connection between a derailment and the quality of the oil in a working air compressor 2,000 feet from the wheel that left the track, yet this pearl of information made it into the final report. Several of us opined that the age and year of kindergarten of the engineer's daughter had somehow missed inclusion into the report.

Little can move a QA department into the realm of irrelevance faster than information that has nothing to do with the issue. The status of the air compressor oil and countless pearls of useless information sure did for that QA department and the QA manager who now knows the status of the air compressor oil.

What the hell is wrong with admitting that one does not know everything about everything? Even though she's out of QA, years later, she still comes to meetings with three-ring binders full of useless data. Eyes roll and people speed dial each other's cells so folk can pretend there's a crisis and get out of the room.

There is no better way to get the quality message out to the teaming masses than to have a good, tight, relevant presentation full of interesting factoids. If you can, make it fun. One of the worst places to work, in quality or otherwise, is one that takes itself too seriously.

The Nutshell

- The quality assurance staff must be allowed to do QA work. The fact that they are versatile and creative should be used for the quality effort.

- Quality people should be advocates of retaining information for the establishment of useful company history.

- Presentation of quality data must be kept simple and clearly stated.

- We must resist using "special" language charts and graphs that have unique meaning only to those of us in quality.

- Ask a simple question—If I can't describe it and display it for everyone to understand, is it really a problem?

CHAPTER 7

WE IN QUALITY CONTROL
ACTUALLY CAN...CAN'T WE?

Problem # 7—Assuming that wholesale inspection
can make quality happen.

An examination of inspection and quality.

IN THE 60S AND 70S, THE NOTION THAT quality could
be inspected in was prevalent. We bought cars and
damned near everything else, fully expecting it to
do most of what it was expected to do—but not quite
everything. If the headlight on the vacuum cleaner didn't
work, the cord only wound up four times, and the little
rubber belt screamed and broke in a cloud of foul-smelling
rubber smoke every week, well, that's what ya get. Hey,

it came with twenty-five extra belts, didn't it? When the window crank on my 1970 Dodge Duster broke off, I had a friend in the Dodge parts department inform me that they had it under control; they had a bunch of 'em in stock. The one I was given was exactly like the one that broke, and when I pointed this out, was told, "That's the fix; we give you another one and don't even charge you."

It's sad to say, but I think the American workforce, the same one that defeated the Germans and the Japanese, took quality as a joke. Remember the story of the autoworkers on the Detroit line who hung Coke bottles from a string inside the door panel of the car so there would be a random and nearly untraceable clunk in the car when it went around a turn?

I guarantee every car we bought, every radio we plugged in, and every vacuum cleaner we went home with had been inspected. They all worked, at least to the inspection criterion at the plant, but not to what a reasonable person would want.

Harley Davidson was in trouble as the 70s ended. Seven out of ten motorcycles needed one to three hours of repair to even operate just after coming off the assembly line. Every ad for a used Harley always had the line "top end, just re-done." One of the founders, William Harley, had a grandson, also a William, who refused to give up. With the help of investors, he bought the company back from AMF and got the employees together. He told every machinist, painter, harness builder, assembler, and probably the janitors that if quality didn't go into the second-gear spur before it left their bench, quality couldn't go into the transmission. If the metal wasn't smooth and clean, the paint wouldn't be, either. If the crimps weren't tight on the wiring, the engine would miss, or the lights would flicker. If the plant was a pigsty, quality work couldn't take place. The new Harley owner would be pissed, and they all might lose their jobs.

Everybody got the message. New designs eliminated the "top end, just re-done" line from re-sale ads. Workers produced bikes that started and ran right off the line and then for a long damned time. The Harley factory paint shop is rated better than nearly all the custom shops, their everyday production work lasts and looks good for years, and if you can get a plant tour, you'll see a place where pride and craftsmanship can take place; it is neat, clean, and orderly. There's even a name for this shop philosophy, it's 5-S, and we'll talk more about it later.

This, combined with a truly committed ethic of connecting and staying connected with their customers has brought them away from the bankruptcy cliff and into the ranks of well run and profitable companies. So, where's the QC at Harley? Yes, some people do QC specifically, but it's more for outsourced material than what's built inside HD. Everybody is QC. Everybody can reject a component, no matter who made it.

As Harley-Davidson found out, empowerment of the individual is the most powerful, economical, and productive type of QC. Period.

Rebuild Inspection vs. New Manufacture QC

In one of the shops I supervised, I had a union worker assigned to do a limited QC on every part we rebuilt. We rebuilt everything that had a wire going to it at a transit company. Several hundred different things to be re-done, and what we put out was, in many cases, better than new. The instructions for my QC people were simple: check over the component. If a problem was found, call the worker who did the re-build, and get it fixed. I was not as worried about what worker had the problem as that a defect didn't leave the shop. I got a report later on any problems found, and in a general meeting, we all discussed ways to improve. Isn't inspection of re-built parts in conflict with the title of this chapter? Not really. There's a big difference in re-manufacturing processes and building new ones. Processes, by their nature, cannot be stabilized as well in a re-build shop. Each item re-built in the shop I managed was looked at. If employee "A" had never had an issue with the power cam controllers they built, the QC person would move their unit quickly. Problem workers got a closer look. Union rules and lack of senior management backbone limited my latitude in "motivating" problematic employees. Remember the Pareto Principal? 20% of something takes 80% of the rest, so in a shop with 68 employees about 13 were various degrees of a pain in the ass, the other 55 were downright awesome.

Over the past thirty years, I have purchased a dozen or so re-built starters and alternators for the cars I have owned. Not a damned one has worked on the first try. I do not buy re-built components anymore. Those re-build guys need this book!

So it's a fact that it's not possible for a process to be as effective for a re-build shop as for a new product. In this sixty-eight-person shop, the worker doing the re-build did most in-process inspections. Self-inspection never works as we would like. Production lines that rely on self-inspection without empowerment, which is problematic in a union environment, are bound to have processes that cannot be stabilized. Another issue with this particular shop was the wide range of things we re-built. If it had a wire going to it and wasn't a printed circuit board, we fixed it—even the refrigerator in the lunchroom!

I used the QC bench as the data collection point for how we could improve the overall shop process. We worked together to find where the time consuming and repetitive work was done, and got entry-level helpers to do those things.

As an example, metal cleaning was automated to a tub-type tumbler, and painting processes were streamlined and done for the whole shop by the helpers. As for the inevitable conflicts with the QC person when they found something that a worker thought was perfect, my position was simple—I will always back up the QC guy. Yes, even if they are wrong. I'll correct them later, in private, if necessary. The shop workers understood this, and the problem never came up in three years and tens of thousands of re-built components.

In this shop, if a component got to the field and a quality problem was encountered when the part was being installed, I would get the QC guy and the person who did the re-build and go to the site, dropping everything to see what the problem was. In every trip we went out on, not a single problem was ours. Yes, delivery and packaging was sometimes at fault and improved, and instruction on how the part should be used and installed was done, and we would have "owned" the problem if we were responsible. A negative was turned into a positive. I admit not many of us can go where the things we made are found lacking, but can't we complete a well—done NCR and CC that information to our workers? Consider for a moment how powerful a morale-building tool it is to have your employees validated in front of their end user. It was a delight to see how good they felt when their supervisor backed them up as quality workers.

After about a dozen trips, the calls ended. The users didn't want to deflect a problem to others that was actually theirs. We still gave out repair parts without casting blame. It's more important to have the thing work than to find who might be at fault. That job is for others, not quality.

I believe, and the data backs me up, that in the service and manufacturing arenas, inspection should be done in process, but not by the people doing the work. Have QC look at the gears going into the robot, not trying to figure why it scratches its butt when it should be painting the items on the production line. See how your technician placed the air conditioner, not why he needed an extra six miles of tubing and eighty-three pounds of Freon to reach and charge it.

Once a process is in place and delivering a repeatable product, inspection can be backed down. I do not agree with some of the military AQL (acceptable quality level) formulae. I'm skeptical of a cookie cutter application of anything, especially quality. The switch that says the baggage door is closed and locked on a Boeing 757 is more important than the one that says the gas filler door on your Cadillac is shut, therefore the inspection and testing of the airplane part should be more extensive than the car part, even if they are built on the same line, by the same people, with the same parts. AQLs would tend to treat them the same.

The Nutshell

- Wholesale inspection to achieve quality does not work.

- Whenever possible, involve those with the quality problem in the resolution. This is an important step in empowerment of the workforce.

- Production lines that rely on self-inspection without empowerment, which is problematic in a union environment, are bound to have a process that cannot be stabilized.

- Self-inspection is the worst form of QC and never works because it flies in the face of human nature, and has never been documented as a stable process.

- Empowerment of the employee for enforcement of quality will pay quality dividends for years.

CHAPTER 8

FEAR AND QUALITY

Problem #8—Employees fear the management. Fear must be driven from the company, quality and those doing it.

D R. EDWARDS DEMING WROTE THAT WE MUST DRIVE fear out of the company. He's right, of course. Fear stops ideas faster than a TSA airport screener stops someone with a flame-thrower strapped to his back. It has always amazed me when I see managers work to have their employees fear them – yes, I've seen and worked for managers who worked hard to instill fear in their subordinates. How then could good ideas and new thinking come up from the workers? The biggest way this is manifested is by making some outrageous rule (like no reading newspapers on the lunch break) and then picking some unlucky schmuck to "make an example of." Yes, I have worked for managers who should be feared. They were nuts. But the worst managers were just plain evil. If you ever see eyes with no conscience and no shadow of morality, buddy, that's scary.

I was a senior instructor for maintenance at a major transit company. The Director of training called me in and said without a tinge of remorse, "I don't like Sam. Fire him." She had been the advocate for hiring Sam in the first place. My refusal to fire Sam without cause cost me that position and nearly my career in transportation.

Another company hired a new CEO who came with a reputation of requiring loyalty and strict implementation of his direction. He normally had great ideas, but on a tour of one of the rail yards, he made the off-handed comment that it looked like there was too much inventory. Within a week, tens of millions of dollars of new stuff, most made special for the company, was thrown into dumpsters and carted away. As the items were needed, they had to be purchased again at higher prices. No one could overcome their fear of the new man's reputation and make the case for keeping the inventory (or even a part of it).

Irrational fear must go.

As mentioned before, if QA people are misused to render problems through unwarranted inspection, audits of paperwork, and artificial performance standards targeted at specific supervisors or their workers, it begets fear of the QA group. The QA staff must never be seen as management's undercover police force, and if present when we arrive or are promoted into a QA position, we must end it. This is a personal hill I will fight on, and I suggest everyone should too. Basic human dignity requires that we can go to work, do the job we were hired to do, and do so without fear or harassment. Okay, I'm off the soap box.

As a supervisor, I was marked down on my performance review because I hadn't written up enough people. Pointing out that unscheduled absences for my crew was lower than any other group, that the waiting list to get into my shop was the longest in the union's history, and that production was up 12% didn't matter. I feared the review process. Any feared process in a company is counterproductive and must be eliminated.

I've been told that I have the dubious talent of delivering bad news without being seen as a bad guy. I have to be careful because I'm a big guy—nearly 6"4' and 250 pounds. I had to learn to lessen my size and perceived power in communication, especially when the news is bad. This is called "marketing a communication" by the folks who study this stuff. Most of us resist the idea of marketing an idea or thought as a cop-out. I would argue that, if it's important to be heard, and if our ideas precipitate actions, then marketing is another tool to get the point across. Those who know us instinctively know when we are serious, but many don't, and they need our marketing efforts.

We in quality are in the idea business. We motivate the company to make whatever we make better, and then better again, and if not better, cheaper with no loss in quality. We need to move the stagnant green water and get it clear again. Quality can make the difference in layoffs and new hires. Okay, back on the soap box again. How do we get people to buy into the notion of CQI? We must eliminate the fear of change.

Several things can help. Producing solid benchmarking data showing that our competitors are moving forward while we are stuck in the "same old's" is a good one. If the bulk of our workforce is male, the idea that others are doing it better tugs at a basic competitive instinct.

Women like to win, too, but their competitive nature demands a different approach. Studies have shown that most women are more concerned with the good of the whole than success of the individual, which may account for humans surviving as long as we have on this war-ravaged, disease-ridden, lunatic-tolerating rock. Suggesting that the company is in more jeopardy if the competitors move forward while we stay static is a powerful motivator for women.

You may have run into a few exceptions. I've had a few woman managers who felt they needed to adopt the killer instincts they perceived successful male managers as having. Bullies and ass-xxxxx have no gender and should not be copied. The two best managers I've ever worked for were women, so was the worst. When we try to emulate what we perceive as a good trait, it often gets magnified, like a feature of someone's face in a cartoon caricature.

Look, this marketing thing can get awfully esoteric. It's valuable, though, and I suggest looking at the work of two authors on the subject. My point is less specific than what Dr. John Grey says in *Men Are from Mars, Women Are from Venus*, and Georgetown University's linguist Dr. Debora Tannen writes in her excellent book *You Just Don't Understand: Women and Men in Conversation*. We need a way to be heard by the audience we are trying to convince. It's marketing our communication. Don't we all feel fearful when we leave a meeting with no understanding of the tasks outlined in there? Isn't it hard to fear someone who's communicating well, and has spoken to us as equals?

Another tactic for removing fear is to involve the workforce in setting the standard for the expected level of quality we are looking for as outlined in Chapter 3. Isn't it hard to fear those who need and want our input?

Using the specification and the PO (if it has useful data), ask the workers to give the QC standard. It is human nature to select a standard higher than the work they are doing. Often, I've been in the position of interjecting, "Yeah, but what if?" into the discussion to bring their lofty ideal quality into the realm of possibility. Once this is done, moving to the next level is easier. Empowerment of the workers drives away the fear of standards and change because they are working with processes they helped create.

In the shop I described a few chapters ago, I challenged the workers to find a better way to do what they do, even if it cost a million bucks. Most were not used to thinking outside the shop, much less outside a theoretical box, but not all. We tried several dozen ideas, most of which didn't work. The ones that failed were supported as they ran their course as much as the ones that succeeded.

We had to try all of our new ideas undercover, even the improvements to the physical shop in which we worked. The managers above us were so afraid of trying something that didn't work out that they stopped movement every time they got wind of an experiment. They were working for the fear driven Assistant General Manager. Quality professionals can't let dinosaurs stop them from moving forward, and it's easier to ask forgiveness than permission. We should not fear a failed attempt at CQI; our fellow workers will see this lack of <u>our</u> fear and lose theirs as well. If movement is to happen, who better than QA to facilitate it?

Fear of change, fear of inspection, fear of competition, fear of being told we are not doing it well enough, fear to attempt change—all fear must be dealt with.

All fear must go.

The Nutshell

- Nothing can affect quality more than fear of those managing a company, or those working to assure the quality of a product; therefore, fear of management must go.

- Nothing can keep problems simmering until they explode more than fear of telling those in management or quality there's a problem; therefore, fear of upward communication must go.

- Nothing can stop thinking and trying new ideas more than the fear of consequences for failure of an idea to work; therefore, managers at all levels must empower everyone in the company to work for CQI. Fear of failure when trying and implementing new ideas must go.

- Related to the bullet above, fear of change must be driven out of the corporate mindset. Those with whom we are competing are not standing still and will run us down when they lap us; therefore, fear of change must be eliminated.

CHAPTER 9

QUALITY ASSURANCE AND PROGRAM OVERSIGHT

Problem # 9—Allowing program management to run its own project oversight.

BUSINESS IS GOOD, GREAT, IN FACT! IT'S TIME to expand, and there's room for new construction on the west side of the plant. There's a problem. You are in the floating candle polecat incense business—not much relation to a million square foot factory construction project. The accountants suggest hiring a "procurement specific program manager" to oversee the construction—planning to commission.

The committee selects a PM. She's a go-getter and negotiates a bonus for on time finishing of the work, and a bigger one if done early. She points out that she'll need a small staff to do the QC and QA for the main building and the polecat rendering equipment, which must be specially made.

The scenario above is not far out of line with a bunch of big-ticket procurements I have worked on. Let's see where the problems are.

We should never agree to a bonus for doing what we are hiring the person for.

We should be very wary of bonuses for finishing a major project early, especially if there are no penalties for finishing late. Remember, we hired them to oversee an area where we have no internal expertise. Isn't it asking a lot for a PM to get the best quality, even if that means forfeiture of a healthy bonus? What possible reason would a PM jeopardize their early out with extra bucks if quality issues are covered up, won't show up for several years, and can be "expedited"? Such was the case of a project for a company I work with in which an entire layer of rubber roofing on a shop was omitted. No problem—until the snow had time to saturate the insulation, which held enough water to cause it to rain inside the shop for weeks.

As stated several times, having QA and QC for a project overseen by the ones who will benefit from finishing it early is a conflict of interest.

I agree that the PM should be able to hire some QA and QC for the job. It's irresponsible for any company to hire people for a job and terminate them when the job's done. There is no problem with hiring job-duration people as consultants; it saves RIFs and layoffs later. But how can we protect the interests of the company, especially if the family jewels are entrusted to hired guns?

Might I humbly suggest having properly placed and budgeted onboard QA staff take on an overseer role? They know the needs of the customers. If properly included in the planning process, they have the needs and background to know what's entailed. A good QA person does not need to know anything about construction to take an oversight role. Audits are audits and can be examined to see if they meet a specified criterion. The PM's QC inspectors will create documentation that can be perused. It's human nature for an inspector to approach his job with a great deal of gusto; this normally tapers off as projects go into weeks and months, but should they? That should be an area of oversight for the in-house QA.

On one troublesome project I worked as QA oversight, the project inspectors were told not to make waves, that their findings were "advisory" only, therefore did not need to be documented. My QA partner and I put a stop to that in a hurry. Advisory? What the hell is that? Yeah, it's way out of specification, and we admit you found it, but we probably won't fix it? What a crock!

It does not normally take a lot of time for QA people to develop oversight processes that can give snapshots of the progress of the project. This isn't always so, however. In another instance, the builder of some expensive equipment got out of control, delivery schedules ran late, and the equipment delivered did not work. The first delivery was used as spare parts for the second and third units, and soon the yard was full of stuff that didn't work. Months into the procurement, in-house QA got involved with the project QA on our own, and against every PM on the project. We got some backing from the people providing part of the capital money. We shut down the contractor's factory for six weeks and made them demonstrate a stable process for every step of the build. When we allowed production to re-start, units came in, passed testing, went online, and began making money.

The time involved in getting the project in line was about six months for three QA officers, about 1/3 of their time—less than a couple hundred grand. Not bad for a $280,000,000 buy. Unfortunately, we were not compensated for getting the production process stabilized. Poopies! Should we have been? See the next chapter.

The Nutshell

- Quality assurance should be used in an oversight capacity when outside consultants and/ or program management is spending the company's money.

- Those being overseen must not control this over–sight.

- All special-project QA and QC should be told that their work is open and transparent to company quality assurance personnel.

- Quality assurance tasked with the oversight must be made aware of any bonuses attached to the contract, who receives them, and what must be accomplished to get the money.

CHAPTER 10

IS YOUR QUALITY ASSURANCE
A MONEY PIT?

Problem # 10—The quality assurance group does
not recover the cost of quality.

A
S A SOURCE INSPECTOR, I HAVE TAKEN
AIRPLANES across the country, stayed in hotels,
eaten meals at the government's per-diem rate,
and arrived at the factory in a rental car, only to find that
the vendor was not ready for inspection. I suggested to
my client that they not pay for the next trip to complete
the inspection. Their answer was that they had no legal
recourse since the contract did not make provisions for
such a contingency. It should have!

The auto industry has several ways in which the quality
assurance group is reimbursed for quality failures of

vendors. A good friend of mine actually got the Daimler-Chrysler M-class QA into the black. They were reimbursed for wasted trips every time. While desirable, it's unusual. In the next few pages, we will look at ways Quality can bill for the issues it has.

In the previous chapter, we saw where an out-of-control contractor should have paid a part of the QA budget. We should be ready and willing to park QA people at the problem factory to get minute-by-minute information on their efforts to correct their processes. These could be people from consultant companies, or even someone from internal assembly areas.

The point here is that the expenses should be borne by the problem vendor. If we find the need to cancel our contract, we have data as to why the vendor has been moved to the "disqualified" list. The legal department loves that.

What happens when quality is working?
Who pays for QA then?

When I worked in maintenance, I got into many an argument with management about my workers "wasting time" reading or playing crossword puzzles. If the shop was clean, the supplies were stocked, and there were no items in the queue waiting for repair, what's the problem? Did my boss want something to break down? Did he want failures affecting the customers just so we had something to do? If the maintenance people are up to date and the things they are responsible for are working, it's probably a good day.

As a firefighter, I scolded the young firefighters who moped around waiting for the alarm. I pointed out that when the bell went off, someone's day had gotten worse, maybe forever. A good week for me was one in which the fickle finger of fate missed the people we were tasked with protecting. Sometimes we have to pay for things we hope will never be used. When things are going well, recovering the cost of quality presents more of a challenge.

My point here is that, like a well run maintenance operation, if we are producing good quality and can prove it, there may be a cost associated with the QA branch. Isn't it more than offset by the lack of rejects and returns? I support the management's right and obligation to suggest QA prove it is on top of the processes and working for continuous quality improvement. But are we finding successes in quality? Have we ever considered the cost benefit of really trying to find people doing it right? Do we shy away from carrying and waving the quality flag? Are we walking the quality walk? A well crafted letter commending workers for a job well done is worth more than we may ever know. Finding people doing what they say and are paid to do should never be overlooked.

That said, when is the last time we did an internal audit to look for opportunities to increase profit, or reduce risk?

Is there a place where we can get into the Quality Toolbox and maybe do a Six-Sigma exercise? One client had been maintaining busses for 80 years in 4 shops across the city. On a mandated Federal Transit Administration inspection one shop did a bus in 8 hours, and another took 29 hours for the same inspection. The other 2 shops were somewhere in the middle. All can't exist in the same universe of busses and be true.

I suggested that the problem be examined by the DMAIC Six-Sigma process. Whole college semesters are given on DMAIC but here's what we did:

- D = Define the problem—shops should be consistent within reason for the time to inspect and service a bus.

- M = Measure—what is to actually be done on the required inspection?

- A = Analyze—what is consistent in the shops and what can be done to make all shops be able to perform the inspections to a standard and within a time frame acceptable to the needs of the fleet and management?

- I = Improve—in the case of the bus inspections, one area was set aside for all inspections, all needed parts for the inspection were placed in this area, engineering created a checklist which allowed all interior stuff to be inspected before the bus was raised in the air (which took 10 minutes, up and 10 down, which was done 6 or 7 times using the old process.

- C = Control the process—this was done by getting the union buy-in. Workers were told that they had 8 hours to do an inspection, repairs would be done later from work-orders they created. If they got done early, and the supplies were up to date, area cleaned, they did not have to start another job.

This was a classic use of DMAIC and Six-Sigma, and saved hundreds of thousands of dollars a year, and brought the company into FTA compliance for the first time in 30 years! Obviously DMAIC and Six-Sigma principals don't need to be done for all projects, but look around. Is this something your QA person or staff could be doing. By the way, portions of this also qualify as LEAN six-Sigma, especially the bringing of all the shop supplies to the location where they are used, saving time workers had to go to the stock-room for light bulbs and oil filters Etc.

In most small, moderate to mid-sized companies, there are plenty of opportunities for quality to be improved. It's sometimes hard to see where opportunities might be lurking. I suggest we step back from the table for a minute and look at what costs money in our QA operation. The results of this introspection might surprise us. In my example at the beginning of this chapter, I painted a picture of a cost incurred by one of the subs in the wasted trip. But if we look at the service and manufacturing sections of our own company as our quality customers, they may be the ones to take the monetary hit when a quality problem needs attention.

As a quality officer, I inspected trains that had completed scheduled periodic inspection and maintenance (PI). They had a higher rate of failure than vehicles that had been out of PI for several weeks—many failures within hours of the completion of the PI. Failure analysis pointed us to areas where scheduled maintenance was actually causing problems. As a QA group, we worked with the maintainer staff. These mostly low-seniority people did not know the interaction of their slice of the maintenance pie with the overall operation of the vehicle. This QA fieldwork caused failures to slow, and in some cases to stop by pointing out problems with the PI process.

In a good operation, the QA group would have gotten the data from the QC or other operations folk. Using the QA section to do the inspections was a big mistake. It's been my experience—countless others have echoed it—that the people finding the problem may not be the best in fixing it. This was true in the PI example above. If a mechanic who was also the inspector found a brake pad or motor brush worn to the minimum length, he could either change it, or take a chance on it lasting until the next PI. If the day was really hot, or really cold, or he was hung over, I guarantee the pad or motor brushes would wait. QC inspectors inspecting, and mechanics doing the mechanical stuff is the best way to implement periodic maintenance. This is the way aircraft are repaired and inspected.

In the scenario, where QA was under the train inspecting, I suggest creating an internal process to move money from budget to budget. Put in place a way to internally bill the scheduled maintenance budget, shifting the cost of the actual QA (most of which was really QC) work back to the customer receiving the benefit. Companies should also consider ways to charge for training and educating the workforce by the quality staff.

Simply considering the QA and QC functions as overhead is misplaced unless the QA staff is doing other value-added work, like preparing the company for ISO registration, or Federal or other externally mandated compliance. Even if this is the case, QA money should be moved from other budgets. ISO registration and Gap analysis should be a separate budget line item. It costs most companies big $$$ to become ISO registered; the business side of professional Quality makes it so.

Quality as a money saver

I have been less than impressed with the record of many companies in their inclusion of QA in the procurement process, either on the buyer side or as a vendor. Having the QA group involved in any company's major purchase or sale makes good economic sense. It has been my experience, however, that program management is unwilling to include quality in these negotiations. I don't know why other than as mentioned in Problem #2, quality is seen by less than savvy PM's as an impediment. Assuring that we can provide our customers with a specified quality delivered at the end of a stabilized process is a powerful sales lever. For a purchaser, knowing that the vendor can do the above is insurance that we will get the product we are requiring, on time and to the specification.

I'd like all reading this to consider manufacturing's motivation to get it right if part of their operating budget is deflected to another department when that outside department comes in and cleans up their problem. Think of how quickly a vendor gets their processes in line when your company's QA people are in the plant looking at every step of their internal process at a billable hourly rate. If our business is service, consider the leverage on the service workforce if they never know if the customer they are visiting is a "blind consumer" QA guy in drag, noting how the service call went and the professionalism of the service people on site.

Recovering the cost of quality is more than an obvious improvement of the bottom line; it's one of the best ways to move toward continuous quality improvement.

The Nutshell

- The quality assurance section of a company should be given ways to bill their customers, internal and out, for their services.

- Time and resources for benchmarking should be a cost associated with marketing.

- Auditing of processes should be a function and expense of production set-up.

- Pre-shipment inspections of outsourced components should be part of the overhead budget built into the original PO or contract.

- Quality oversight should be a line item in the project budget being overseen.

- Quality troubleshooting of an unstable process should be billed to the area of service or production where the out of control process was discovered and corrected.

- ISO preparation, Gap analysis, transitional auditing, and auditing for external compliance should be budgeted separately from the regular QA overhead.

- If a quality assurance section cannot show real work toward CQI, they should have a budgetary consequence, just like all the other quality customers.

CONCLUSION

I HOPE THIS EXAMINATION OF QUALITY HAS BEEN HELPFUL. I do not agree with the notion that we are small quality fish in a big manufacturing pond. I think we have not been good enough at selling the quality message to the fish swimming around us. If we don't adopt better ways to market our message, it's our fault.

I believe everyone wants to do a better job, make a better thing, or make a thing better. It's human nature. We in quality are movers toward this human desire to be better. Those we encounter who do not have this instinct have most likely had it beaten out of them by the afore–mentioned dinosaurs. If we search the metaphorical souls of workers and managers, we can awaken that dormant will to do "it" better and then even better again. We can find the good inside workers who have become complacent, set in their ways, and lazy, and start motivating them to get back in the game.

Our job is easier if we are properly placed in the company and insulated from manufacturing and delivery pressures, but if we aren't, we still have an obligation to try. It is easier to work for a company where the managers are not stuck in the 60s, but some are, and we have to either get to them, or go around them.

Results are difficult to ignore.

We have to be ready to allow quality to happen without our name being on the plaque handed out in the semi-yearly quality assembly. Many times, I have given data to the dinosaur to present as his. As people committed to quality, who gets the credit is less important than having the company in a position to give out that credit. If we are able to convince those around us that Quality is not just a good word, but also a real thing that can assure we have jobs to go to and products that people desire, we have succeeded. If we have people around us running from one quality fire to another, either we have lost, or we need to figure a better way to get the message out there.

The stakes are simply too high to fail.

GLOSSARY

OF SOME QUALITY TERMS

Affinity Diagramming—Collecting ideas and placing them in groups of related thoughts, normally after charting a brainstorming session.

Brainstorming—Getting everyone in a room and writing down every idea surrounding a topic. A way to get buy in from a group of otherwise disinterested people.

CEO–Chief Executive Officer—The top person in management residing at the company in question—in this book OWNER, CFO, and CEO are synonymous.

Containment—limiting a Quality problem to specific boundaries using traceability to limit the numbers of effected items. If no traceability, no containment.

CQI–Continuous Quality Improvement—The reason quality assurance exists. A continuous movement toward the betterment of a product or service, or the bottom line.

Dinosaurs—Those in our company who have settled into their comfort zone, often not realizing the glacier is moving toward our company. Those people who always have a reason why new ideas should not be tried, or new systems examined. They disregard benchmarked information as a power grab, and critical analysis as a problem started by malcontents. In the case of dinosaurs in our company, we should hope for the comet.

DMAIC–(duh-MAY-ick) Define the problem—Measure the problem, assess the resistance to change – Analyze the problem, find root causes and ways to eliminate them—Improve the situation, in spite of the dinosaurs—Control the dinosaurs.

Dr. Edwards Deming—The savior of Japanese industry. The most concise proponent of quality theory to ever work in the field of quality.

Empowerment—In this book, a management strategy to allow free thinking in the workplace, specifically directed toward Continuous Quality Improvement.

FAI–First Article Inspection—The first piece of a specified item ordered which will set the Quality standard benchmark for the rest of the run.

ISO—A Quality system developed in Europe as an attempt to standardize the method of assuring quality in manufacturing or service. Most subscribe to ISO 9001, now updated to ISO 2015.

Multi-voting—True democracy as applied to Quality. Everyone votes on the answer to a quality concern. If the voters are populated by idiots, the idiotic answer wins. Kind of like all politics.

Pareto—A dead French bean-counter who came up with the theory that 20% of something takes 80% of the effort, money, or energy to accomplish. Pareto charts are used to identify areas where attention is required. Most Pareto charts are not worth the time and effort to create them if the target audience is not fully conversant with the principal.

QA–Quality Assurance—A system in place to assure a specified level of quality is produced in a consistent, repeatable manner.

QC–Quality Control—A system in place to assure process is followed to assure the desired Quality of an item is in place.

Quality—The specified level of quality delivered by our company.

Quality Circles—A quality system popular in the 80's that concentrated the quality of a product with groups of people from various areas of the process into teams which controlled the quality effort. The most successful were John Deer and Harley Davidson. Other companies failed because the system was discontinued too soon.

Quality Standard—The agreed level of quality deemed acceptable, and is then documented.

Scatter Chart—A way of diagramming where quality action events take place in the manufacturing processes. As an example, if a large number of events (dots) appear in the shipping area of the chart, then efforts to eliminate that area of the Quality problem can be attempted.

SIPOC—A diagramming process–Suppliers–those we get product from, internal or external Inputs–where supplies are used in the Process(s) the instruction governing the operations we do <u>O</u>utput(s)–the last direct step of the process we have control over and <u>C</u>ustomers–the users of out outputs, either internal or external.

Six-Sigma—"Black-belts," "Green Belts," and a series of provisional status levels of certification allowing for more hierarchy in the six-sigma system. A quality system based on the dissection of the standard deviation sine curve. Removing error to the sixth standard deviation, allowing for no more than 3.14 errors per million intersections of a Quality event.

Lean Six-Sigma—Lean systems eliminate waste in time and worker activities. Items are in the workstation, parts used are within reach of the worker. Tools and equipment are near where they will be used. Proper Lean systems can save a company huge amounts of money.

Risk—the term associated with all forms of risk associated to a particular product or service, and for the Quality Assurance discussion, is all risk, internal and external.

Stakeholder—The theoretical person who has an interest in the outcome of a quality system.

Traceability—The ability of management to determine the origin and time of creation of any product or service we provide. Proper quality oversight requires traceability.

TQM–Total Quality Management—A system of certification that focuses on the "big quality picture" rather than the details of the quality system. This system uses esoteric definitions to allow for global thinking of company processes.

QUICK

INTERNAL AUDIT

CHECKLIST

Frye – rev-new
3/3/2019

The questions in this sample audit are designed to find out the current status of a company's current Quality System, and point out where improvement is needed. Internal Audits can be general, like this one, or specific to an identified problem area. Notice the questions move around some, this keeps the auditor and auditees thinking more generally, not linearly. This gives more true answers and keeps auditees from saying what they think the auditor wants to hear. Also be aware each question is just a guide for the auditor, and each answer can generate another set of questions not on the checklist. The exception to additional questions is if several companies are being audited (not an internal audit) then each MUST be asked exactly the same questions.

1. If asked, any employee can say who in the company is the Quality Assurance person?

   Ans_____

   a. If asked, any employee will acknowledge that they can suggest ways to improve quality, profit, or processes

      Ans_____

   b. If asked, any employee can describe who they can go to for a question regarding quality issues.

      Ans_____

2. Can any employee can tell the auditor what the Company Quality policy is, and where the Quality Assurance manual is and how they can access it?

   Ans_____

3. Can any manager, supervisor or lead-person describe the procedures for correcting a quality issue brought to them by workers?

   Ans_____

4. Are work instruction, processes, or checklists available for workers to use to perform their task (this includes field workers doing service work)?

   Ans_____

a. Are instructions in good condition, in the language of the worker?

Ans_____

b. Do work instructions have rev. levels, and authorized signatures?

Ans_____

c. Are part numbers for specific parts on the work instruction?

Ans_____

d. Are any special processes noted?

Ans_____

5. Do purchase orders have sufficient information to assure the correct part is being ordered?

Ans_____

6. Are any instructions for incoming inspection of received parts on the purchase order?

Ans_____

7. Does your parts department/area have a strict first-in first-out policy?

Ans_____

8. Is there a policy for issuing a Supplier Corrective Action Request (SCAR)?

Ans_____

9. Is there a clearly understood Non-Conforming Report policy in place?

   Ans_____

   a. Does it have a clear definition of the root cause analysis?

      Ans_____

   b. Does the policy designate who can declare a NCR closed?

      Ans_____

   c. NCR process for Material?

      Ans_____

   d. NCR process for correcting a manufacturing processes?

      Ans_____

10. Is there a procedure for processing rejected materials?

    Ans_____

11. Is there a segregated, locked, controlled location for rejected parts?

    Ans_____

12. Is the Quality Assurance reporting chain outside of purchasing and manufacturing?

    Ans_____

13. Does the CEO, Owner or highest manager at the location demonstrate by actions that they support Continuous Quality Improvement?

Ans_____

14. Is there a method of revising procedures that assures all affected processes and people are brought up to date with the changes?

Ans_____

15. Who is responsible for Quality?

Ans_____

16. Who is responsible for Continuous Quality Improvement?

Ans_____